The MAILBOX®

W9-AYM-486

LET'S DO Science Today!

Step-by-step investigations that build science process skills

- Observing
- Describing
- Discussing
- Asking questions
- Comparing
- Connecting
- Predicting and more!

Plus follow-up activities and reproducibles!

Managing Editor: Gerri Primak

Editorial Team: Becky S. Andrews, Diane Badden, Kimberley Bruck, Karen A. Brudnak, Kitty Campbell, Pam Crane, Chris Curry, Lynette Dickerson, Lynn Drolet, Tazmen Hansen, Marsha Heim, Lori Z. Henry, Lucia Kemp Henry, Amy Kirtley-Hill, Debra Liverman, Dorothy C. McKinney, Thad H. McLaurin, Brenda Miner, Sharon Murphy, Jennifer Nunn, Mark Rainey, Greg D. Rieves, Hope Rodgers, Leanne Swinson, Zane Williard

www.themailbox.com

Manufactured in the United States
10 9 8 7 6 5 4 3 2 1

Table of Contents

What's Inside

Easy to Plan and Prepare

Take the steps with you! Simply tear out the page and slip it inside a plastic protector!

Easy to Lead

Recording Sheets

Easy to Carry Out and Extend

Extension Activities

Key Science Learning
A noise seems to sound different depending on how close or far away it is.

During the investigation, students

- use the sense of hearing to make observations
- describe sounds as loud or quiet
- listen to sounds from different distances
- predict which item makes a specific sound

Materials:
3 empty, clean snack-size potato chip canisters with lids
construction paper
rice
paper clips
pennies
student copies of page 8

In advance: Cover each canister and lid (if it is transparent) with paper. Number the canisters from 1 to 3. Place a supply of rice in one canister, paper clips in another, and pennies in the last.

Getting Started
Ask students to name loud and quiet sounds.

STEP 1

Gather a small group of students at a table. Stand across the room and gently shake canister 1. Ask students to listen to the sound and tell whether it is loud or quiet.

STEP 2

Give each child a copy of "Listen Up!" Instruct students to check *loud* or *quiet* at the top of the first section of their papers. Then have them write or draw what they think is in the canister.

STEP 3

Ask students, "What can I do to help you hear the sound better?" After accepting several ideas, stand close to the group and gently shake the canister again. Ask students to listen and tell how the sound changed.

STEP 4

Have each child check *loud* or *quiet* at the bottom of the first section of his paper and write or draw what he thinks is in the canister.

STEP 5

It was rice!

Remove the lid and have students look in the canister to check their predictions.

STEP 6

It sounded louder when it was close.

Ask, "Was it easier to hear the sound when it was far away or when it was close?" Guide students to understand that what they hear depends on how close (or far away) they are from where the sound is made. Then repeat the investigation with the remaining canisters.

This Is Why

Sound waves travel outward in all directions from where a sound originates. The sound waves nearest the source of a sound have the most energy, which means a sound seems loudest in this location. As sound waves travel away from the source, they weaken and the sound becomes more difficult to hear.

What Now?

Ask students to name things in the environment that sound very loud when they are up close and sound quieter when far away. Consider things such as trains, airplanes, construction vehicles, or a lawn mower.

More About Sound

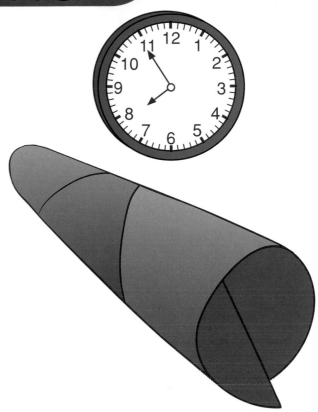

Make It Louder!
Comparing sounds

An ear trumpet makes soft sounds easier to hear. To make individual ear trumpets, help each child roll a sheet of construction paper into a funnel shape and then secure it with tape. Invite each child, in turn, to listen to a quiet sound such as a ticking clock or a radio at a low volume. Then have him hold the narrow end of his ear trumpet close to his ear (without inserting it into the ear) and point the wide end of the trumpet toward the object making the sound. Ask him to compare the sound he heard using the ear trumpet with the sound he heard without it. Guide students to conclude that a noise sounds louder through an ear trumpet because the trumpet guides sound directly into the ear.

Sounding Off
Making and checking predictions

For this small-group activity, label six film containers with numbers from 1 to 6. In each container, place a different material shown on the reproducible on page 9; then secure the lids. Have each group member cut out the picture cards from a copy of page 9. Next, have one child gently shake container 1 and listen to the sound that is made. Then have her pass the container to another child in the group. After each child has taken a turn, ask her to predict the contents of the container by placing the matching picture card on her paper. Repeat the process with each remaining container. Invite students to change their predictions throughout the activity. After the sixth prediction is made, ask them to glue their picture cards in place. To check each prediction, open the container, show students the contents, and help them finish the corresponding sentence on their papers.

Name _____

_____ Sound
Recording sheet

Listen Up!

1

From far away, the sound is
☐ loud ☐ quiet

I think I hear…

From up close, the sound is
☐ loud ☐ quiet

I think I hear…

2

From far away, the sound is
☐ loud ☐ quiet

I think I hear…

From up close, the sound is
☐ loud ☐ quiet

I think I hear…

3

From far away, the sound is
☐ loud ☐ quiet

I think I hear…

From up close, the sound is
☐ loud ☐ quiet

I think I hear…

Let's Do Science Today! • ©The Mailbox® Books • TEC61165

Note to the teacher: Use with "Sounds All Around" on pages 4–6.

Name_____

Shake and Listen!

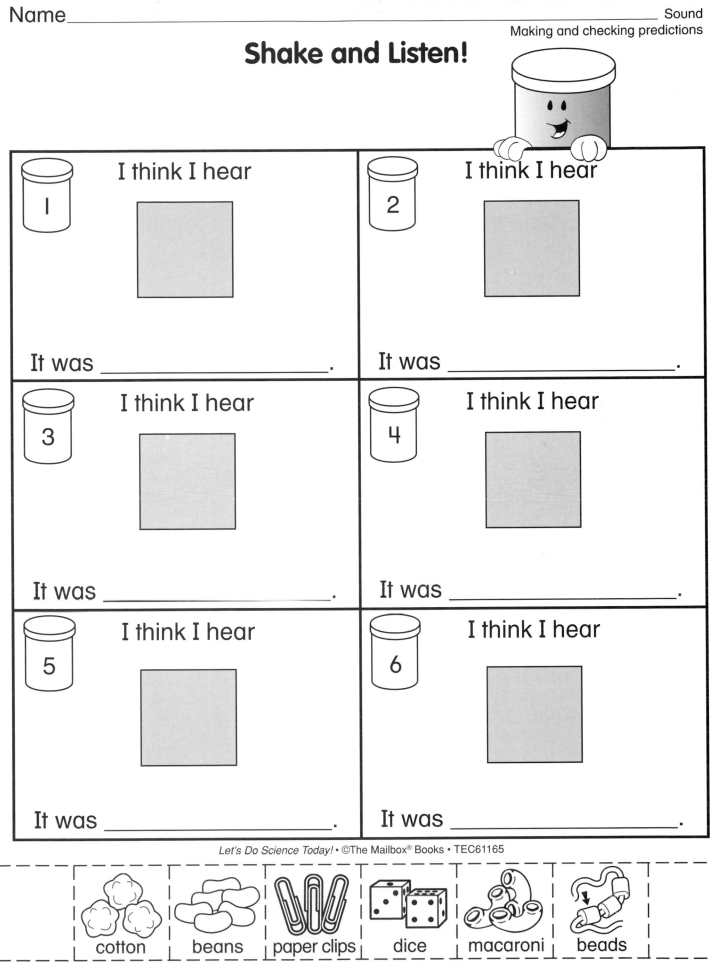

1	I think I hear
It was _____.

| 2 | I think I hear |
It was _____.

| 3 | I think I hear |
It was _____.

| 4 | I think I hear |
It was _____.

| 5 | I think I hear |
It was _____.

| 6 | I think I hear |
It was _____.

Let's Do Science Today! • ©The Mailbox® Books • TEC61165

cotton   beans   paper clips   dice   macaroni   beads

Note to the teacher: Use with "Sounding Off" on page 7.

9

Get in Touch!

Key Science Learning

The sense of touch can be used to identify different properties of objects.

During the investigation, students

- describe properties of objects using the sense of touch
- compare the properties of objects
- make predictions about the identity of hidden objects

Materials:
3 large paper grocery bags
feather, sandpaper, apple, cotton ball, pinecone, plastic egg
student copies of page 14

In advance: Make three touch bags. Begin by cutting a small opening in each paper bag (see Step 2). Then fold forward the top of each bag, staple along the fold, and label the resulting flaps "A," "B," and "C." Place the cotton ball in bag A, the pinecone in bag B, and the plastic egg in bag C.

Getting Started

Ask students to name ways they use their sense of touch.

Investigation
Get in Touch!

STEP 1

This apple is so smooth! The feather is soft.

Gather a small group of students and have them examine the apple, the sandpaper, and the feather. Have students describe each object, leading them to use texture words such as *smooth, rough,* and *soft.*

STEP 2

I felt something small and soft.

Display bag A. Have each child, in turn, reach in the bag and feel the hidden object. Invite students to describe what they felt without saying what the object might be.

STEP 3

I think it's a pom-pom.

Give each child a copy of "Touch and Tell." Have her show on her paper beside bag A what she thinks she felt. Invite students to compare their predictions.

STEP 4

It was very light and fluffy!

Ask, "How did your sense of touch help you make a prediction?" Guide students to name properties that their sense of touch revealed (for example, shape, texture, size, and weight).

Investigation
Get in Touch!

STEP 5

STEP 6

Remove the item from the bag. Have each child check *yes* or *no* to show the outcome of her prediction. If she checked *no,* direct her to complete the sentence.

Have students repeat Steps 1–5 for each remaining bag.

This Is Why

There are millions of tiny nerves under the skin. When these nerves come in contact with an object (or a substance), messages about what is being felt are sent to the brain.

This feels smooth and pointy.

What Now?

Remind students that skin covers the entire body. This means the brain receives lots of messages about what is touched and felt. Challenge students to describe things they have felt with different parts of their bodies, such as wind on their faces or sand between their toes!

I felt my kitty's fur when it rubbed on my leg!

More About Touch

This Feels...
Identifying textures

This hands-on investigation reinforces the connection between touch and texture. Display a variety of items that feel smooth, rough, or soft. Give each child a copy of "Touchable Textures" on page 15. Instruct each student to feel each item, identify its texture, and then write or draw a picture of the item in the corresponding column of his paper. Discuss the students' findings and then encourage them to name items from home that fit in each category.

Name Joshua

Sense of Touch Recording sheet

Touchable Textures

These things feel smooth.	These things feel rough.	These things feel soft.
foil cup	stick	scarf pillow

Test the Water
Making thermal observations

With this activity, youngsters gain an understanding that their sense of touch helps them make decisions and keeps them safe. Fill one bowl with warm water and a second bowl with ice water. Have students feel the water in each bowl and describe its temperature. Invite each child to name something that is hot or cold; then write their responses on a two-column chart. Guide students to understand that skin contains heat and cold receptors that send messages to the brain that help us decide whether to touch an object (or a substance) or move away from it.

Hot	Cold
pizza stove water in the bathtub	ice cubes snow water in the pool

Name _____

Touch and Tell

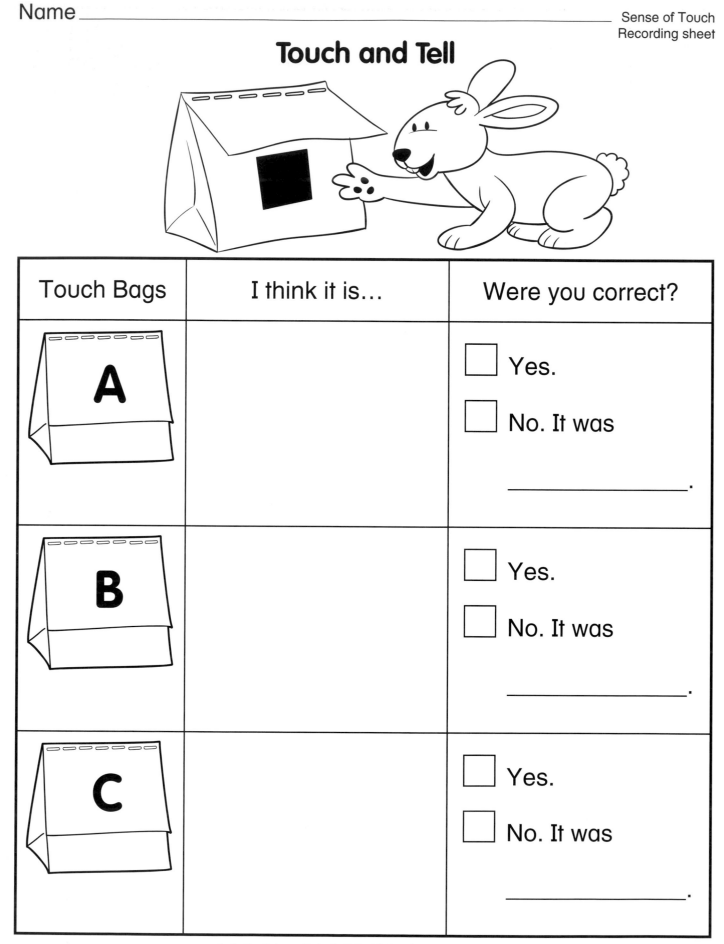

Touch Bags	I think it is...	Were you correct?
A		☐ Yes. ☐ No. It was _____ .
B		☐ Yes. ☐ No. It was _____ .
C		☐ Yes. ☐ No. It was _____ .

Let's Do Science Today! • ©The Mailbox® Books • TEC61165

14   **Note to the teacher:** Use with "Get in Touch!" on pages 11–12.

Touchable Textures

These things feel **smooth**.	These things feel **rough**.	These things feel **soft**.

Note to the teacher: Use with "This Feels…" on page 13.

Use Your Senses!

(Pages 16–21)

Key Science Learning

We use our five senses to gather information.

During the investigation, students

● predict the identity of a concealed food using the senses of hearing and smell

● describe the food using sight, touch, and taste

● write sensory words to describe the food

Materials:
opaque container with lid
pickles
student copies of page 20

In advance: Place the pickles in the container and seal it with the lid. Make a large five-column chart labeled with the words *hearing, smell, sight, touch,* and *taste.*

Getting Started
Find out if students can name the five senses and tell something about each one.

Let's Do Science Today! • ©The Mailbox® Books • TEC61165

STEP 1

We can taste!

Gather a small group of students and explain that they are going to first try to identify a food without using their sense of sight. Have students close their eyes. Ask, "What other senses can you use to investigate?"

STEP 2

It's bumping against the bowl.

Have students, in turn, shake the container and describe what they hear. Write student responses in the corresponding column on the chart. Invite each child to predict what she thinks is in the container.

STEP 3

Yes! It smells like pickles!

Then open the container slightly, but do not reveal its contents. Ask, "Do you think smelling the food can help you identify it? Why or why not?" Have students describe the smell. Record their responses on the chart. Guide students to understand that we get more information when we use more of our senses.

STEP 4

They're all green and bumpy.

Show students the contents of the container. Encourage each child to describe the pickles using color, size, shape, and texture words. Write the responses on the chart.

STEP 5

It tastes sour!

Give each student a pickle and have her describe what it feels like. Invite each child to take a bite of the pickle. Ask, "How is the inside different from the outside?" Have students describe the taste. Record their responses on the chart.

STEP 6

Hearing	Smell	Sight	Touch	Taste
bumping	like pickles stinky	green bumpy	outside is harder than inside	sour

Review the completed chart. Give each student a copy of "Pickle Perceptions." Have her write a descriptive word to complete each sentence and draw a pickle.

This Is Why

Our five senses send messages to our brains about things we see, hear, taste, smell, and touch. Using all five senses helps our brains gather more information.

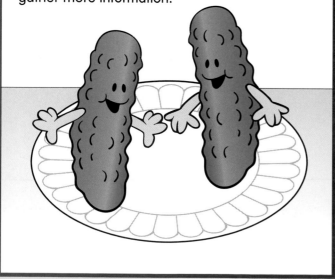

What Now?

Have students predict what is for lunch using only their sense of smell; then compare their predictions to what they see being served. Ask each student to describe the tastes of the foods and compare their descriptions. Then ask students to describe what the foods sound like and feel like as they eat.

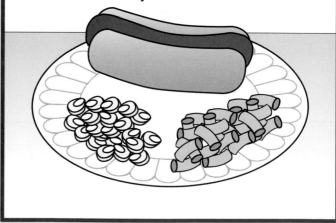

More About The Five Senses

Look-Alikes
Identifying substances

Students use all five senses to identify two similar substances. Label each of two resealable bags "A" and "B" and place salt in one bag and sugar in the other. Instruct students to close their eyes and listen as you shake each bag, in turn, and then try to identify the substances by each sound. Next, have students open their eyes and ask them to describe what they see. After students predict what each item is, give them a sample of each substance to smell and touch. Then invite them to change their predictions if desired. Finally, invite students to taste each substance and identify what each one is.

Guess My Favorite Food
Drawing conclusions

Youngsters use sensory clues to identify a mystery food! Ask each student to think about what her favorite food looks, smells, feels, tastes, and sounds like when eaten. On a copy of "Guess My Favorite Food" on page 21, have each student secretly draw a picture of her favorite food in the box and write the name of the food on the line. Next, help her staple a 3" x 6" piece of paper where indicated and complete the page by writing words to describe the food. Invite each student to exchange her paper with a classmate. Then have each youngster read the clues, guess the mystery food, and lift the paper to verify her answer!

Five Senses
Drawing conclusions

Guess My Favorite Food

ice cream cone

My favorite food

looks **brown**

smells **like chocolate**

sounds **quiet and crunchy** when I eat it.

tastes **yummy**

feels **cold and soft**

Name _____

Pickle Perceptions

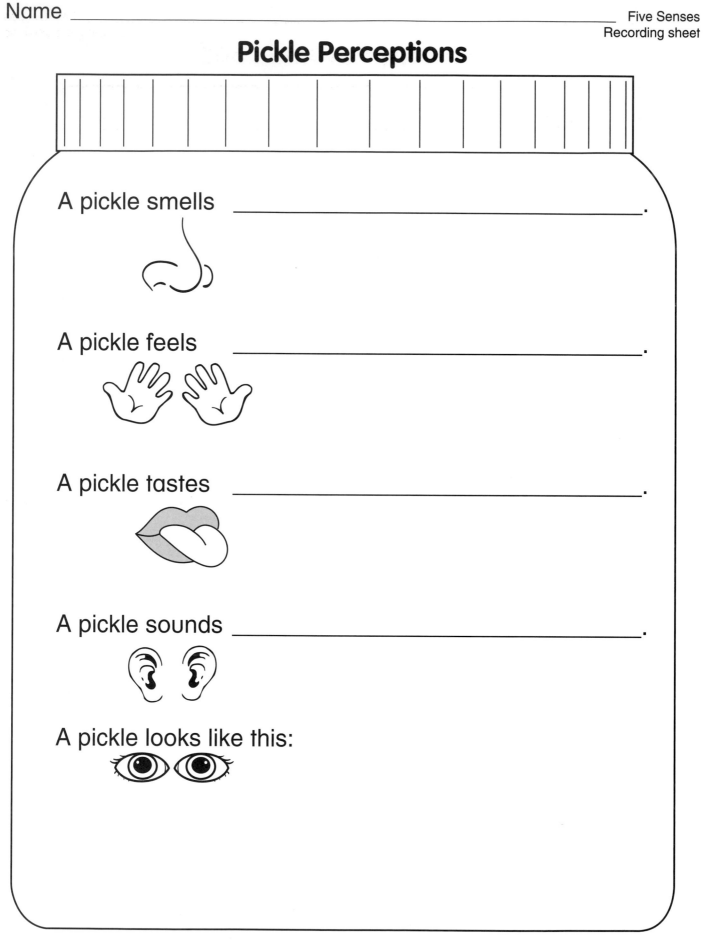

A pickle smells _____ .

A pickle feels _____ .

A pickle tastes _____ .

A pickle sounds _____ .

A pickle looks like this:

Let's Do Science Today! • ©The Mailbox® Books • TEC61165

20   **Note to the teacher:** Use with "Use Your Senses!" on pages 16–18.

Guess My Favorite Food

Name of food: _____

Staple here.

My favorite food

looks _____.

smells _____.

sounds _____ when I eat it.

tastes _____.

feels _____.

Note to the teacher: Use with "Guess My Favorite Food" on page 19.

Living and Nonliving

Key Science Learning

Living things need water, food, and air and use them to grow and change.

During the investigation, students

- examine living and nonliving things
- describe similarities and differences between living and nonliving things
- consider the characteristics of living and nonliving things
- determine whether something is living or nonliving and tell why

Materials:
inflated water toy
plant
class pet (or insect)
play dough
crayons
student copies of page 26

In advance: Display the objects from the materials list. If you do not have a living critter in your room, capture an insect. Be sure to set it free when the investigation has been completed.

Getting Started
Find out what students think is the difference between living and nonliving things.

Investigation
Living and Nonliving

STEP 1

"The plant needs air. The ball has air in it."

Gather a small group of students and have them examine the materials on display. Invite one student to sit by the materials as part of the comparison sample. Ask, "What is the same or different about the objects?"

STEP 2

"Living things need air, food, and water."

"They also grow and change."

Give each child a copy of "Check 'em Off!" Use the checklist to help youngsters identify the characteristics of living things.

STEP 3

"Pencils get smaller. And they don't eat food!"

Lead a discussion to help youngsters conclude that some nonliving things might have one or two of the characteristics, but not all three. Ask, "Can you name something that changes but does not need food or water?"

STEP 4

Recap that living things need food, water, and air; they also grow and change. Then have youngsters look at the display and complete the checklist for each item.

STEP 5

Help youngsters determine whether each item is living or nonliving and have each child circle the correct word for each row. Remind students that all three boxes must be checked if it is a living thing.

STEP 6

Instruct students to work together to sort the materials on display as living or nonliving. Then encourage youngsters to discuss some of the living characteristics that some of the nonliving objects possess.

Did You Know?

Our earth is home to more than ten million living things! Some are huge like blue whales and others are tiny like bacteria.

What Now?

Lead your students outside to identify living and nonliving things in the real world. Challenge youngsters to identify the missing characteristics of the nonliving things.

More About
Living and Nonliving

Sorting It!
Identifying living and nonliving things

Label a class-size chart "Living" and "Nonliving." Then instruct students to cut out a variety of pictures that show living and nonliving things. Have each child sort the pictures and post them on the corresponding side of the chart. To review, have each child, in turn, select one of her pictures and explain why the object is living or nonliving.

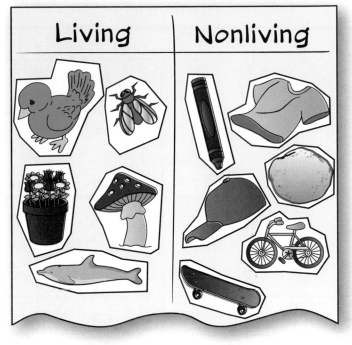

Nonliving Necessities
Identifying nonliving things

Some items may not be living, but they sure are useful! Pose the question "What nonliving things do you use every day?" Help each student write a response on his own sheet of paper. Then ask him to illustrate his paper. After each child shares his page with the class, bind the completed pages into a class book. If desired, make another book featuring the needs and uses associated with living things.

Check 'em Off!

✔ Check all that apply.
Circle to show whether each object is living or nonliving.

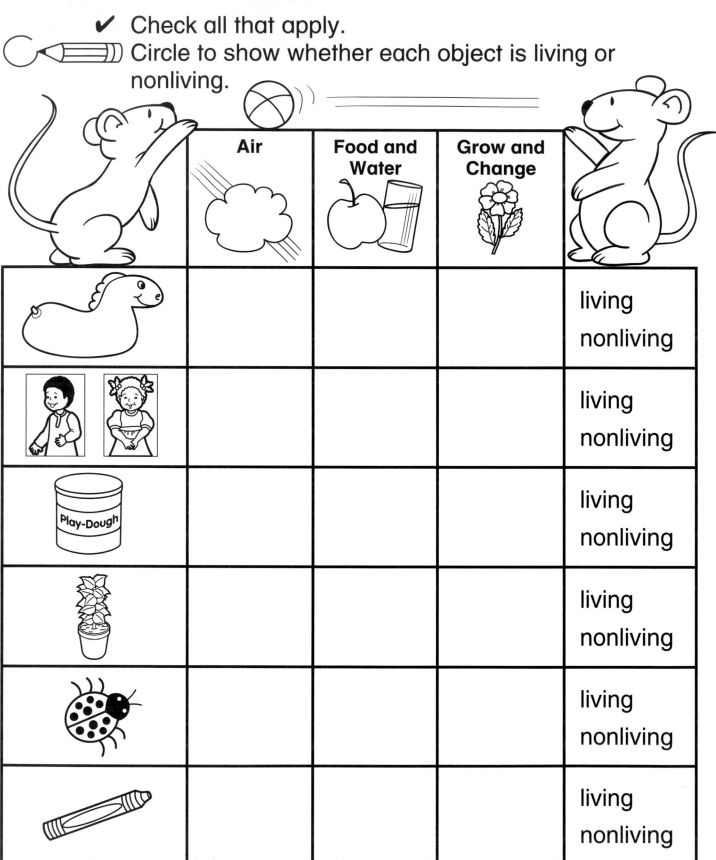

	Air	Food and Water	Grow and Change	
				living nonliving
				living nonliving
Play-Dough				living nonliving
				living nonliving
				living nonliving
				living nonliving

Let's Do Science Today! • ©The Mailbox® Books • TEC61165

26   **Note to the teacher:** Use with "Living and Nonliving" on pages 22–24.

Circle the things that need air.

Living things need air.

Circle the things that need food and water.

Living things need food and water.

Living things grow and change.

Circle the things that grow and change.

Living Things Need...

Name _____

Let's Do Science Today! • ©The Mailbox® Books • TEC61165

Fold-and-Go Booklet: To make a booklet, cut on the bold line. Fold along the thin horizontal line (keeping the programming to the outside) and then fold along the thin vertical line (keeping the cover to the outside). Read aloud each booklet page and have each child follow the directions to complete the booklet.

Basic Needs of Plants

Key Science Learning

Plants need water, soil, and sunlight to grow.

Plant A

During the investigation, students

- observe differences in plants
- describe characteristics of healthy plants
- name the basic needs of plants
- identify what plants need and what they do not need

Materials:
thriving plant
neglected plant
student copies of page 32
crayons
scissors
glue

In advance: Label the healthy plant "A" and the neglected plant "B."

Plant B

Getting Started

Find out what students think plants need to live.

Investigation
Basic Needs of Plants

STEP 1

This one looks green. That one looks brown.

Plant A

Plant B

Gather a small group of students and have them examine plants A and B. Have students describe the differences between the two plants.

STEP 2

Sunlight!

Explain that plant A has been on a windowsill and plant B has not. Ask, "What did plant A get on the windowsill that plant B did not get?"

STEP 3

This soil is a little wet.

Plant A

Plant B

Have students touch the soil for each sample. Then ask, "How are the soils different?" Guide students to understand that plants need rich, damp soil.

STEP 4

Water!

Ask, "What did plant A get to make its soil damp that plant B did not get?" Lead youngsters to conclude that plants need water to live.

STEP 5

A plant does not need a bird to grow.

Recap that plants need water, soil, and sunlight to keep healthy. Give each child a copy of "Grow, Grow, Grow!" Help students determine which pictures show what a plant needs to grow.

STEP 6

Challenge youngsters to cut out and glue the pictures to create an environment that is best for growing plants.

Did You Know?

Plants need clean air to grow too. Smoggy, polluted air blocks the sunlight plants need for healthy growth.

COUGH! COUGH!

What Now?

Plants need space to grow! Go outside to observe plants in nature. Help youngsters understand that plants with little space will remain smaller than plants that have room to grow.

Flourishing Flowers

Identifying needs of plants

Students are sure to enjoy this surprise scene after naming the needs of plants! Staple brown paper ovals (seeds) along the bottom of a bulletin board. Then ask students, "What do seeds need to grow?" When soil is named, invite students to help you cover the seeds with brown tissue paper. When water and sunlight are named as needs, post raindrop cutouts and a sun cutout, respectively. At a later time when students are out of the room, add plant cutouts to the board. There's no doubt students will show excitement when they see the simulated growth! Complete the healthy plant environment with student-made flowers.

Raindrop Reference

Sources of water

Showcase plants' water sources on a supersize raindrop cutout! Invite youngsters to name different ways a plant might get water. Write student responses on a raindrop cutout. If desired, create more raindrop charts to list water sources in different land biomes, such as the tundra, forests, and deserts. Post the completed raindrop(s) to display plants' water sources.

rain
hose
cup
sprinkler
watering can

Name _____

Grow, Grow, Grow!

Let's Do Science Today! • ©The Mailbox® Books • TEC61165

bird

rain

sun

butterfly

soil

rocks

Note to the teacher: Use with "Basic Needs of Plants" on pages 28–30.

Name _____

Happy Plant

Write to label.
Draw a healthy plant.

Plants need **water, soil,** and **sunlight** to grow.

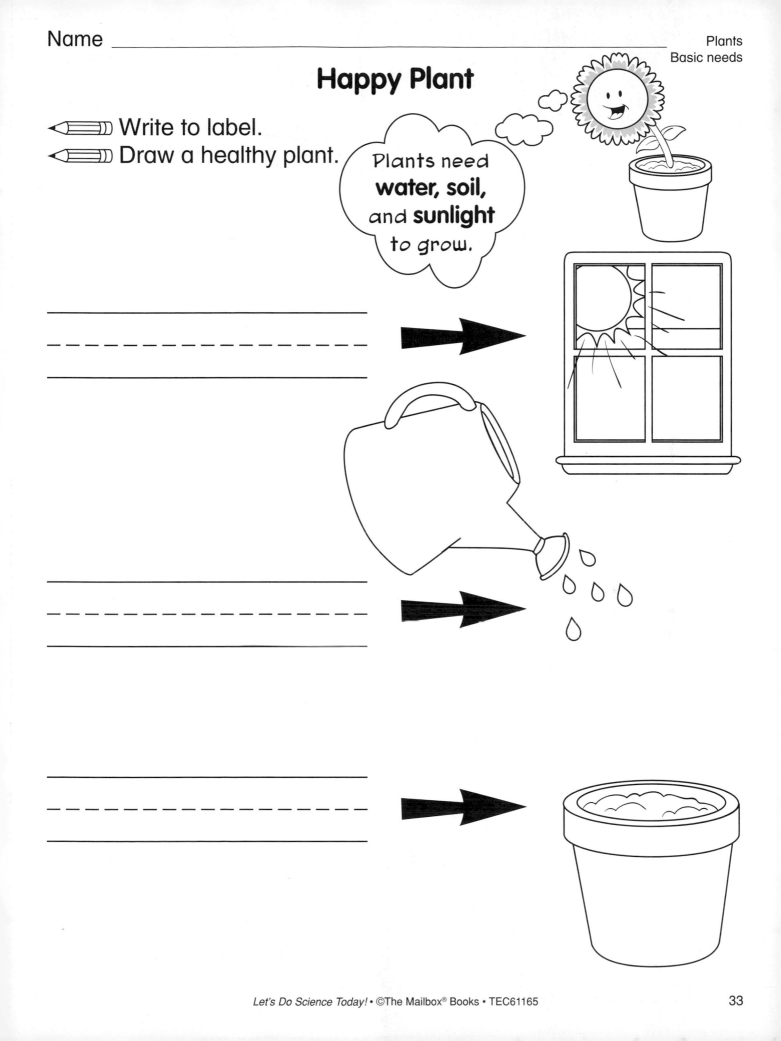

Key Science Learning

Flowering plants are made up of four main parts: roots, stems, leaves, and flowers. Each part helps the plant in a special way.

During the investigation, students

● observe and identify the basic parts of a real plant

● determine the function of each plant part

● match plant parts and their functions on a plant diagram

Materials:
flowering plant
exposed root system
crayons
scissors
glue
student copies of page 38

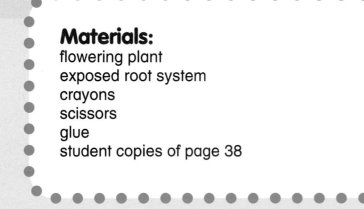

Getting Started
Find out what plant parts students can name *without* observing a plant.

Investigation
Parts of Plants

STEP 1

I see the roots.

Have students examine the flowering plant and the exposed root system. Lead youngsters to name and identify the four main parts of a plant (roots, stems, leaves, flowers).

STEP 2

The roots!

Ask, "What plant part holds the plant in place and takes in water and minerals?" Have youngsters look at the plant, and guide them to discover that the roots perform this function.

STEP 3

That's a stem.

Ask, "What plant part holds up the plant and takes water and minerals to the rest of the plant?" Have youngsters look at the plant, and guide them to discover that the stems perform this function.

STEP 4

I see veins on the leaves.

Ask, "What plant part has veins and takes in sunlight to make food for the plant?" Have youngsters look at the plant, and guide them to discover that the leaves perform this function.

STEP 5

I know pumpkins grow from yellow flowers. Flowers must make seeds and fruits!

Ask, "What plant part grows along the stem and makes seeds and fruits?" Have youngsters look at the plant, and guide them to discover that the flowers perform this function.

STEP 6

Name Juanita
Plant Parts
flower
leaf
stem
root

To review, give each student a copy of "Plant Parts." Have her color the plant and cut out the labels. Then help students read the labels to match each one to the corresponding plant part. When the labels are correct, have youngsters glue them in place.

Did You Know?

Almost all plants spend their entire lives in the same place. Most plants use air, sunlight, and water to make their food. This process is called *photosynthesis.*

What Now?

Go on a nature walk to observe plants in their natural environment. Have students gather fallen leaves as they walk. Then guide youngsters to compare and contrast the leaf collection by looking at the veins, size, and shape of each leaf.

More About
Parts of Plants

Edible Roots, Stems, Leaves, and Flowers!

Parts of a plant

Build on students' knowledge of plant parts with vegetables. Show students a carrot, a stalk of celery, a cabbage leaf, and part of a broccoli head. Lead a discussion about where each vegetable grows and what it looks like. Then have youngsters predict for each vegetable the part of the plant that is eaten. If desired, share photos to confirm that the carrot is a root, the celery stalk is a stem, the cabbage leaf is a leaf, and the broccoli head is flower buds. Finally, encourage youngsters to eat roots, stems, leaves, and flowers for dinner!

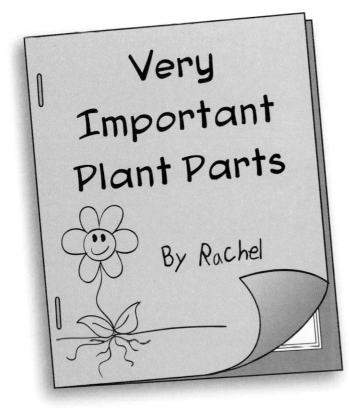

Fact-Filled Reading

Science vocabulary

Here's a riddle booklet that helps students remember plant part terminology! To begin, give each student a copy of page 39, four 2" x 1¼" paper rectangles, and a 6" x 9" piece of construction paper (cover). Have her glue or tape the top of each rectangle to an answer box where indicated and then set the page aside to dry. Direct her to fold the cover in half and write her name and a title on the cover. To complete the booklet, instruct her to cut out the pages and staple them inside the cover.

Name _____

Plant Parts

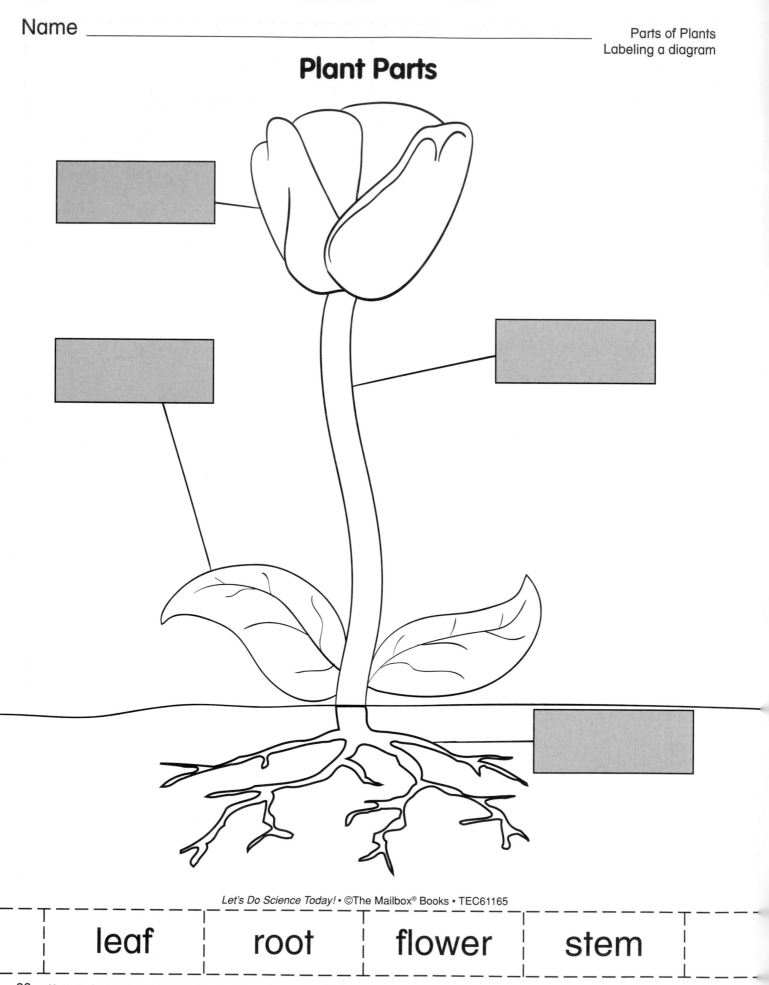

| leaf | root | flower | stem |

38   **Note to the teacher:** Use with "Parts of Plants" on pages 34–36.

I can be colorful.

I make seeds.

I make fruit.

What am I?

Glue.

a flower

I can be tall.

I hold up the plant.

I take water and minerals to the plant.

What am I?

Glue.

a stem

I have veins.

I take in sunlight.

I make food for the plant.

What am I?

Glue.

a leaf

I hold the plant in the ground.

Tiny hairs grow on me to take in water and minerals.

What am I?

Glue.

a root

TEC61165

Note to the teacher: Use with "Fact-Filled Reading" on page 37.

Plants Change and Grow

(Pages 40–45)

Key Science Learning
Plants grow and change over time.

During the investigation, students

- observe a bean plant
- predict how seeds change
- describe the growth of a plant
- record how a plant grows and changes

Materials:
dry lima beans
2 resealable plastic bags
paper towels
water-filled spray bottle
crayons
student copies of page 44

In advance: Wrap several dry lima beans in a moist paper towel, seal the towel in a plastic bag, and label the bag "seven days." Tape the bag to a sunlit window for seven days, misting the towel with water as needed to keep it moist. Prepare a second bag three days prior to the investigation and label it "three days." Save several dry lima beans for the investigation.

Getting Started
Find out what students think about how plants might grow and change over time.

Investigation
Plants Change and Grow

STEP 1

They need water.

They need sunlight too!

Gather a small group of students and show them the dry beans. Explain that the beans are seeds. Ask, "What do these seeds need to grow into plants?"

STEP 2

It might grow roots and a stem.

Have youngsters predict how a seed will change if it gets its basic needs.

STEP 3

They look puffy and a little bigger.

three days

Invite a volunteer to reveal the contents of the bag labeled "three days." Tell students the seeds were kept moist and exposed to sunlight for three days. Ask, "How are these seeds different from the dry seeds?"

STEP 4

I see something long growing.

There's part of a leaf!

seven days

Invite a volunteer to open the remaining bag. Tell youngsters that these seeds had water and sunlight for seven days. Ask, "How are these seeds different from the other seeds?"

Investigation
Plants Change and Grow

STEP 5

Give each child a copy of "Growing Bean Plants" and have her write or draw her observations. Be sure to have her notice how the original seed, the bean, began to transform.

STEP 6

Challenge students to record their predictions of how the seeds will continue to change and grow if planted in the natural environment. Lead youngsters to conclude that plants continue to change and grow over time.

This Is Why

When water is added to the seed, the hard outer shell swells and the seed bursts open. The roots grow and a stem appears that will push the seed upward. Leaves grow on the stem and reach toward the light.

What Now?

Carefully place the bean samples in some soil. Encourage youngsters to take responsibility for the plants and watch them grow! From time to time, compare and contrast the plant growth to individual students' predictions.

More About Plants

All Kinds of Plants
Classifying plants

Compare and contrast different plant life with this class activity. Label a large sheet of chart paper with different types of plants, such as trees, shrubs, flowers, vegetables, and grasses. Then have youngsters cut out plant pictures from gardening magazines and catalogs. Instruct students to glue each picture to the chart under its corresponding label. Use the chart to guide a discussion about the similarities and differences among plants.

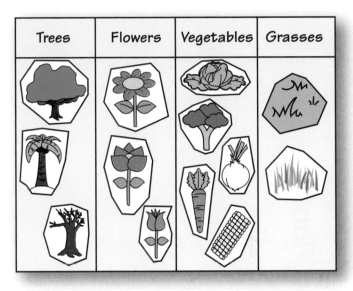

Trees	Flowers	Vegetables	Grasses

Plants give us corn.

Sue

I have a straw hat.

Bobby

We Need Plants!
Plants as a resource

Do humans have an effect on the change and growth of plants? Absolutely! Discuss with students how plants provide people with food, clothing, and shelter. Explain that plants also provide the oxygen in the air that people need to breathe. Then have youngsters write and draw pictures to show how plants help people.

Name _____

44

Growing Bean Plants

I predict...

Dry lima beans:	
3 days with water and sunlight:	
7 days with water and sunlight:	

Let's Do Science Today! • ©The Mailbox® Books • TEC61165

Note to the teacher: Use with "Plants Change and Grow" on pages 40–42.

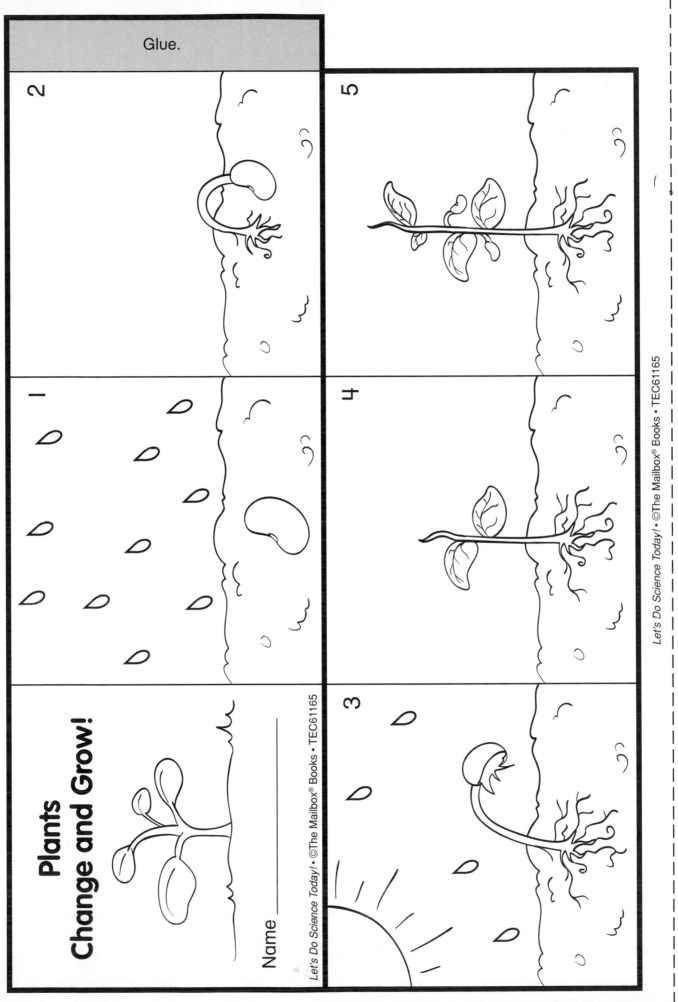

Glue.

2

5

1

4

Plants
Change and Grow!

Name _____

3

Let's Do Science Today! • ©The Mailbox® Books • TEC61165

Let's Do Science Today! • ©The Mailbox® Books • TEC61165

Accordion-Folded Booklet: To make a booklet, cut on the bold lines. Glue the left edge of page 3 to the tab. Keeping the cover on top, accordion-fold the resulting strip to see how plants change and grow over time.

Gotta Have Soil
(Pages 46–51)

Key Science Learning
Soil is an important natural resource.

Soil B

Soil A

During the investigation, students

● observe differences in soil

● draw pictures of observations

● describe a property of soil

● consider why some soil is

  better for plant growth

Materials:
topsoil (or potting soil)
sandy/rocky dirt
2 seedling cups (with drainage holes)
2 shallow containers
water
crayons
student copies of "Dig In!" (page 50)

In advance: Label the seedling cups "A" and "B."
Set the cups in a shallow container, and partially
fill each one with a different soil sample.

Getting Started
Find out if students think all soil is the same.

STEP 1

Gather a small group of students and have them examine soil samples A and B. Have students describe the differences between the two soils.

STEP 2

Give each child a copy of "Dig In!" Show students the line in each box. Instruct students to color soil below each line, doing their best to make each soil look like the sample they examined.

STEP 3

Recap that not all soils look the same. Then ask, "How else might soils be different?"

STEP 4

Choose a different volunteer to pour a small amount of water over each soil sample. Have students describe what they see happening and conclude that this is another way that soils can be different.

STEP 5

Plants!

Ask, "When does it matter whether soil holds water?" Guide students to connect soil and a plant's need for water.

STEP 6

Challenge students to decide which soil sample is better for growing plants, and then instruct each child to color a healthy plant on his paper in the corresponding type of soil.

This Is Why

Some differences in soil can be seen and some cannot. A soil that absorbs water is often desirable for plant growth because plants need water to grow.

What Now?

Find out how many students like to eat watermelon. Help students understand that, because a watermelon needs soil to grow, they rely on soil too. Ask students to suggest other ways they count on soil.

More About Soil

Take a Turn
Descriptive words

Publishing your youngsters' soil-related observations as a class poem is quick and easy. Title a length of bulletin board paper "Soil Is…" Invite each child to take a turn suggesting a word that describes soil. List the words below the title. Have each child sign the completed poem, and display it on a classroom wall.

Soil is...

Abul
Jory
brown
tiny
dirty
good
Fun
everywhere
interesting
deep
Ethan
Tesa
Rose
Nia
Leah
Jake

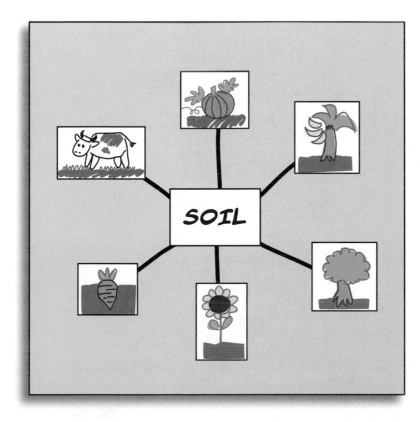

SOIL

Picture This
Soil as a resource

This activity produces a colorful diagram that reminds students how much they depend on soil. Begin by brainstorming with your students things that need soil to grow. Then ask each youngster to color on drawing paper a picture that shows soil and something she enjoys because of soil. Display the student drawings and the word *soil* as shown.

Dig In!

Soil A   ## Soil B

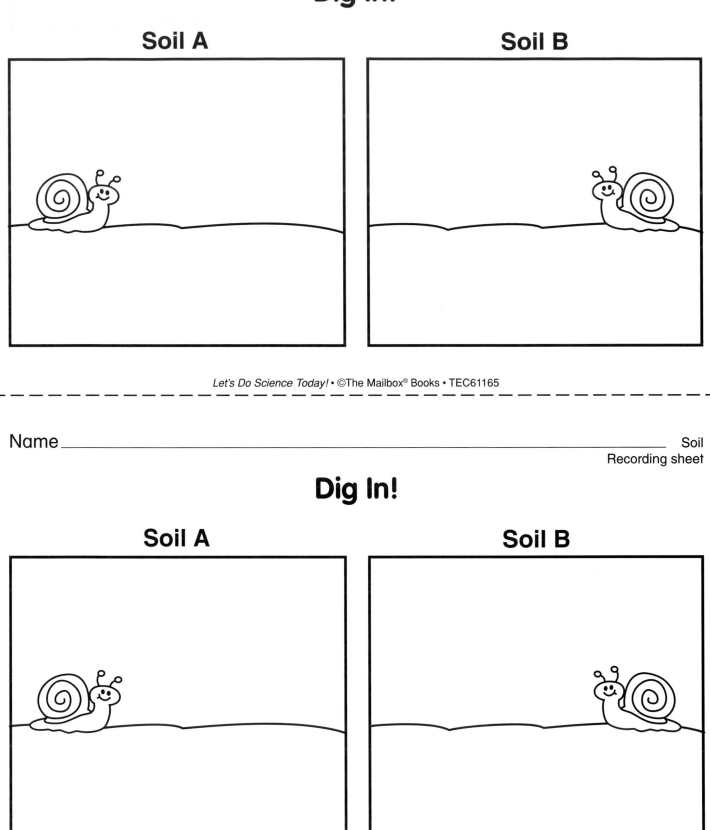

Dig In!

Soil A   ## Soil B

Cross out two!

rocks   cars
trees   plants

Soil helps these things grow.

It rhymes with do.

Cross out one.

brown   red
blue   black

Soil is different colors.

Some animals live in the soil.

Cross out one.

elephants
chipmunks
groundhogs
earthworms

More About Soil!

Name _____

Fold-and-Go Booklet: To make a booklet, cut on the bold line. Fold along the thin horizontal line (keeping the programming to the outside) and then fold along the thin vertical line (keeping the cover to the outside). Read aloud each booklet page and have each child follow the directions to complete his booklet.

The Water Cycle
(Pages 52–57)

Key Science Learning
Water moves and changes in the water cycle.

During the investigation, students

- describe differences in simulated rain samples
- describe the sun's effects on water
- consider how water condenses and precipitates
- conclude that we cannot see all forms of water as it moves and changes in the water cycle

Materials:
2 tubs with dry rocks
filled watering can
2 water-saturated cotton balls
crayons
student copies of page 56

In advance: Label the tubs "A" and "B." The day before the investigation, gather students around tub A. Use the watering can to sprinkle the rocks with water, simulating rain. Encourage students to share their observations. Then place the tub by a sunny window.

Getting Started
Find out where students think the water in a puddle goes as it gets smaller.

Investigation
The Water Cycle

STEP 1

"The rocks were shiny and wet."

Gather a small group of students and ask, "What do you remember about the rocks we poured water over yesterday?" After students share their comments, invite a volunteer to pour water over tub B.

STEP 2

"Today's rocks are wet. Yesterday's rocks are dry!"

Place tub A next to tub B and have students examine the two rock samples. Ask, "Do yesterday's rocks in tub A look the same as today's rocks in tub B?" Guide students to understand the sun's effect on the dry rocks.

STEP 3

Give each child a copy of "Water All Around." Instruct students to draw a sun in the sky. Then say, "The sun dries up the rain, but the water does not disappear."

STEP 4

Explain that the sun's heat changes the water into vapor that we cannot see. The water vapor rises into the air. Instruct students to draw thin lines to represent the vapor we cannot see.

STEP 5

Discuss with students how water vapor cools as it rises and collects in the sky. Introduce the cotton balls and explain that as the water gathers, clouds start to form. Invite two volunteers to each take a cotton ball (cloud), make them drift toward each other, and make them touch, forcing water droplets to fall.

STEP 6

Guide students to understand that when a cloud is too full, the water droplets eventually fall down to the ground. Have each child draw a cloud and rain (or snow) on her paper to complete the water cycle. Then invite a volunteer to use her paper to help her explain how water changes and moves in the water cycle.

This Is Why

Heat causes water to rise into the air as water vapor. The water vapor cools the air as it rises. As the air cools, the vapor condenses and forms tiny droplets of water that we see as clouds. When the droplets become too heavy for the cloud to hold, they fall down to the earth as rain if it is warm or snow if it is cold.

What Now?

Develop students' science vocabulary by having each child complete the booklet on page 57. For each word introduced—*evaporation, condensation,* and *precipitation*—have students color the corresponding picture.

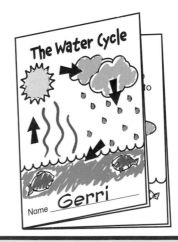

The Life of a Raindrop
Dramatization of the water cycle

Students are sure to enjoy acting out the way water moves in the water cycle! Place large paper clouds, raindrops, and a pond shape on the floor to create a water cycle scene. Then invite small groups of students to act out how they might feel and where they would go as water drops moving through the water cycle. For instance, when a student (raindrop) is in the pond he might be swimming around happily until he gets very hot. In his next move, he might slither or hop up toward the clouds to show evaporation. When students (raindrops) fill a cloud shape, they could animate falling or drifting down as rain or snow.

Poetic Review
Water changes forms

Chant this rhyme to reinforce water cycle concepts.

Evaporation, simply put,
Is water rising to the sky.
As vapor, it is a gas
And you don't see it going by.

Condensation starts to happen
After water vapor rises high.
When the droplets start to gather,
We see clouds up in the sky.

Billions of the droplets
Start to fall and this we know,
It's called precipitation.
It's often seen as rain or snow.

This cycle remains constant.
No, it does not have an end.
The fallen rain, hail, sleet, or snow
Will be on the move again!

Name _____

Water All Around

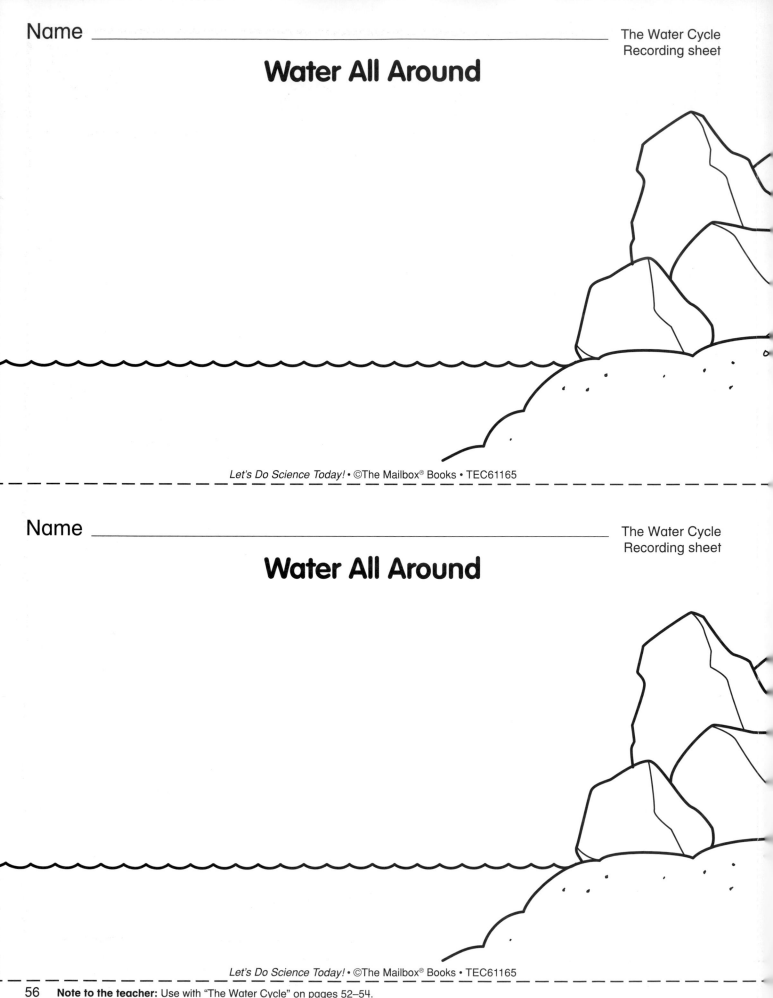

- -

Name _____

Water All Around

Note to the teacher: Use with "The Water Cycle" on pages 52–54.

Condensation
This happens when water vapor cools and forms little drops of water that gather to make clouds.

Evaporation
This happens when the sun heats water and changes it into a gas that we cannot see. The gas is called water vapor.

Precipitation
This happens when the water in clouds falls back to the earth as rain or snow.

The Water Cycle

Name _____

Fold-and-Go Booklet: To make a booklet, cut on the bold line. Fold along the thin horizontal line (keeping the programming to the outside) and then fold along the thin vertical line (keeping the cover to the outside). Read aloud each booklet page and have each child color the corresponding part of the water cycle.

Key Science Learning

Water as a solid has a shape, but as a liquid, it does not have its own shape.

During the investigation, students

- examine water as a solid and as a liquid
- consider the different shapes, or lack thereof, of water
- observe ice as it melts
- conclude that water as a liquid does not have a shape

Materials:
clear cup
clear cup with water
5 red- or blue-tinted ice cubes
plastic spoon
crayons
student copies of page 62

In advance: Put the ice in the empty clear cup and label it "A." Label the cup of water "B."

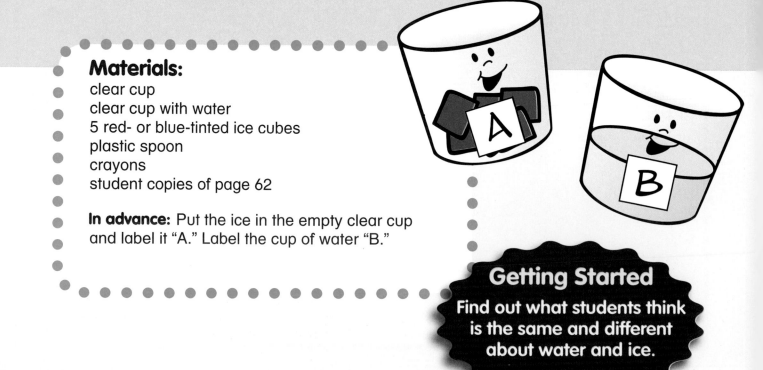

Getting Started

Find out what students think is the same and different about water and ice.

Investigation
Water: Solid and Liquid

STEP 1

There is air in this cup.

All the water is at the bottom.

Gather a small group of students and have them examine cups A and B. Explain that the water we drink is a liquid and when water freezes, it becomes a solid. Have students describe the differences between the water samples.

STEP 2

Give each child a copy of "A Chilling Observation." Instruct students to draw on each of the first two cups, doing their best to make each cup look like the sample they examined.

STEP 3

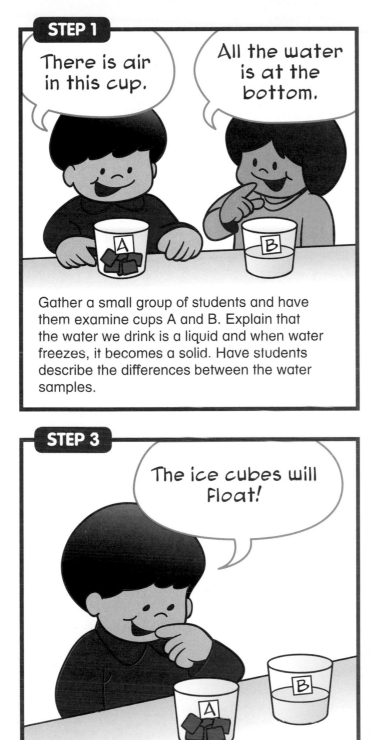

The ice cubes will float!

Have students make predictions. Ask, "What do you think will happen when we pour the water into the cup of ice?"

STEP 4

Invite a student to pour cup B over the ice in cup A. Then have volunteers, in turn, stir the mixture. Instruct youngsters to observe what happens in the cup.

Investigation
Water: Solid and Liquid

STEP 5

The water turned blue.

The ice cubes melted.

Ask, "What happened to the ice and water in the cup?" Guide youngsters to understand that when a solid melts, it loses its shape.

STEP 6

Challenge youngsters to explain why the water is blue. Then have students record their observations on the last cup of "A Chilling Observation."

This Is Why

Solids don't change shape easily. They have to be heated or cooled, pushed or pulled. Liquids can flow. They take the shape of whatever they are in.

What Now?

Find out what students think will happen if you pour the water out of the cup. Lead youngsters to conclude that a liquid takes the shape of its container, or it spreads out all over!

Puddles on Plates

Exploring water as a solid and as a liquid

Students observe ice as it melts and compare the resulting puddles during this activity. Give each child an ice cube on a plastic-coated plate. Have her trace around the ice cube to show its size and shape. Encourage youngsters to share their observations as the ice changes from a solid to a liquid. As each cube melts completely, have the student trace around the resulting puddle. Then have her wipe away the water and put her puddle shape on display. Students are sure to notice the different shapes water can make on these posted plates!

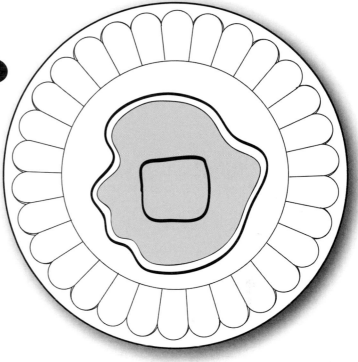

Super Slushy

Following directions

With a few fun shakes, students help change the appearance of a liquid! Help each child pour a half cup of Kool-Aid drink in a resealable sandwich bag and seal it. Then have her put it in a larger resealable bag. Next, ask her to half-fill the larger bag with ice, pour in one-third cup of rock salt, and finish filling the bag with more ice. Help her seal the larger bag. For the next three to four minutes, have her shake the bag. To enjoy this slushy treat, have her remove the Kool-Aid bag, dry it off, get a spoon, and dig in!

Rock Salt

Name _____

Recording sheet

A Chilling Observation

solid

liquid

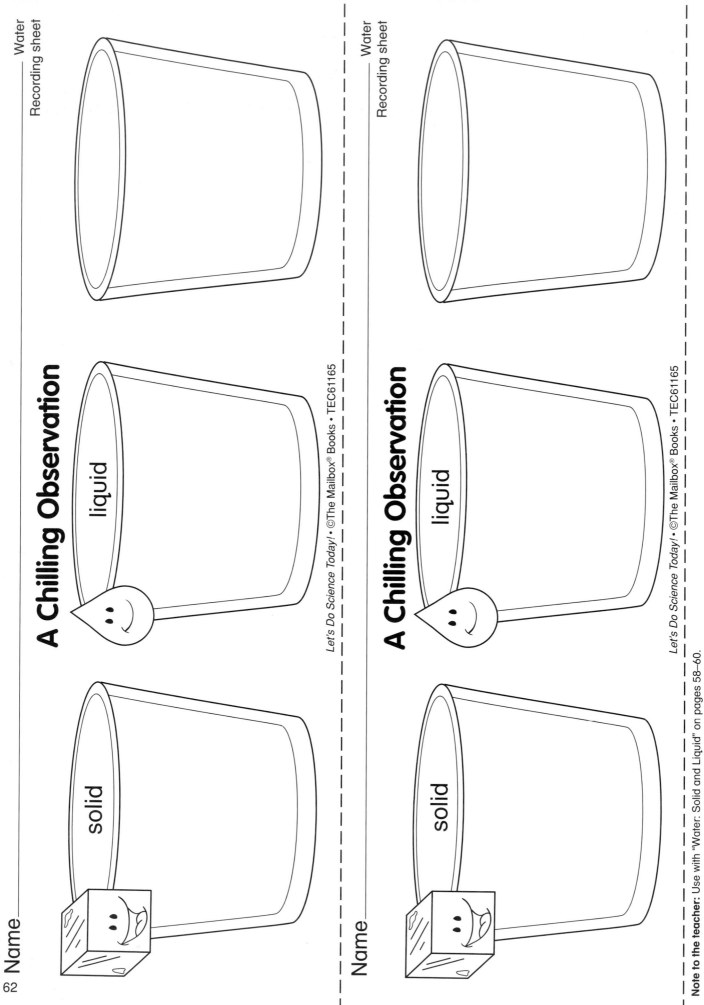

Let's Do Science Today! • ©The Mailbox® Books • TEC61165

Name _____

Water
Recording sheet

A Chilling Observation

solid

liquid

Let's Do Science Today! • ©The Mailbox® Books • TEC61165

Note to the teacher: Use with "Water: Solid and Liquid" on pages 58–60.

Name_____

Water Forms

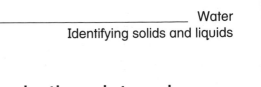 Circle to show whether the water in the picture is a solid or a liquid.

solid   **liquid**

solid   liquid   solid   liquid

solid   liquid   solid   liquid

solid   liquid   solid   liquid

Sink or Float
(Pages 64–69)

Key Science Learning
Many factors contribute to an object's ability to float.

During the investigation, students

● predict whether different objects will sink or float

● consider whether the weight or size of an object determines whether it will sink or float

● observe varying sink/float results using the same materials

● conclude that the size, weight, and shape of different materials affect their ability to float

Materials:
large bowl of water
piece of aluminum foil
pennies
crayons
scissors
glue
personalized class supply of craft sticks
student copies of page 68

In advance: Have each youngster color a copy of the prediction cards. Then have him cut out the cards and glue them, back-to-back, to his craft stick.

Getting Started
Find out why students think some objects sink and others float.

Sink or Float

STEP 1

I think it will float.

Discuss students' reasoning concerning whether the piece of foil will sink or float when placed in the water. Have each youngster hold his prediction card prop with his prediction facing out. Then place the foil in the water. Compare its ability to float to students' predictions.

STEP 2

I predict they will both sink because the penny will make the foil go down with it.

Tell students that the weight of an object can be a factor of its ability to float. Then release a penny in the water. After it sinks, remove the penny. Ask, "What do you think will happen if I place the penny on the foil?"

STEP 3

They float!

Gently place the penny on the foil. After confirming that it floats, revisit students' predictions and discuss reasons why the two materials did not sink. Guide students to realize that the heavier object remained above water when placed on the lightweight piece of foil.

STEP 4

This time it did sink.

Remove the materials from the bowl. Fold the foil around the penny. Ask, "Do you think the wrapped penny will sink or float?" Have each youngster lift his card to show his prediction before releasing it in the water.

STEP 5

The foil stayed at the bottom this time!

Unwrap the penny and release the flattened foil in the water. Place the penny on the foil. Then ask, "What do you think will happen if we place more pennies on the foil?" Conduct the experiment several times for students to make sink and float discoveries.

STEP 6

Remove the pennies and the foil. Curve up the edges of the foil to make a simple boat shape. Then invite volunteers to gently release a penny, one at a time, in the boat. Lead youngsters to conclude that the boat shape held more pennies than the flat piece of foil before sinking.

This Is Why

The water is pushing up against the foil to help it float on the water. When a single penny is placed on the foil, the size and weight remain balanced enough for the water to continue to support both objects. Air also helps an object float. The curved edges of the boat shape gave the water more to push against and trapped air inside it; that's why the boat shape held more weight.

What Now?

Release a small sponge in a bowl of water to see it float. Invite a volunteer to squeeze the sponge while holding it underwater. Tell youngsters that the bubbles are the result of air being squeezed out of the sponge. Keeping the sponge underwater, have the student let it go to see it sink. Guide students to conclude that the air had helped the sponge float. Then remove the sponge from the bowl and squeeze out the water (allowing air in). When placed on the water, it will float again!

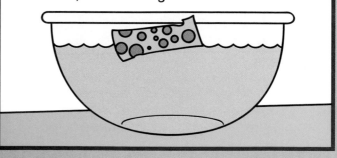

More About
Sink or Float

Shape Matters!

Exploring sink or float with different shapes

A ball of play dough is perfect for sink and float exploration. Have each member of your small group roll play dough into a ball. Instruct her to release it into a tub of water. After it sinks, ask her to remove it and pat it dry. Next, have her mold the play dough into different shapes—such as a thin log, a thick log, a raft, and a boat—to discover how the shape of an object changes its ability to float (buoyancy). Challenge youngsters to explain why various formations made of the same substance have different sink or float results.

My boat has a wide bottom. The water pushes on it to keep it afloat.

Fruit Soup

Exploring buoyancy

In advance, cut a variety of fresh fruit into bite-size pieces. Give each youngster a bowl partially filled with apple juice. Have her predict which fruits will sink and which will float. Then ask her to spoon one piece of each fruit at a time into her bowl. Instruct her to record her results on a copy of "Fun With Fruit" on page 69. Next, lead a discussion comparing and contrasting the results while students eat their sweet treats.

Float

Sink

TEC61165

Float

Sink

TEC61165

Let's Do Science Today! • ©The Mailbox® Books • TEC61165

Fun With Fruit

✏ Draw your observations.

This fruit sinks.

This fruit floats.

Let's Do Science Today! • ©The Mailbox® Books • TEC61165

Note to the teacher: Use with "Fruit Soup" on page 67.

Magnificent Magnets!

(Pages 70–75)

Key Science Learning

Magnets are attracted to some metals, but not all.

During the investigation, students

- compare and contrast a variety of magnets
- examine objects made from magnetic and non-magnetic materials
- make predictions and test ideas
- draw and write to show predictions and outcomes

Materials:
variety of magnets (bar, disk, horseshoe, wand)
magnetic materials such as a paper clip, a nail, a safety pin, and a washer
nonmagnetic materials such as a dime, a rubber band, a toothpick, and aluminum foil
student copies of page 74

Getting Started

Find out what kind of objects students think magnets are attracted to.

Investigation
Magnificent Magnets!

STEP 1

Some magnets are bigger.

Gather a small group of students and have them examine the magnets. Invite each child to describe the similarities and differences between the magnets.

STEP 2

This is a paper clip. It's made from metal.

Invite each child to examine the collection of objects made from magnetic and nonmagnetic materials. Have students identify the objects and name the material they think each object is made from.

STEP 3

The paper clip and dime will stick to a magnet.

Give each student a copy of "Magnetic Attraction." Have her show in each column an object from the collection that she predicts a magnet will be attracted to. Invite students to share their predictions.

STEP 4

Yes! The dime didn't stick to the magnet!

Instruct each student to choose a magnet and use it to test her predictions. Ask, "Did anything surprise you when you tested your predictions?" Have each child check the corresponding boxes on her paper to show the outcome of her investigation.

Investigation
Magnificent Magnets!

STEP 5

The dime isn't the kind of metal that sticks to a magnet!

Remind students that magnets are attracted to certain metals. Ask, "If the paper clip and the dime are both metal, why do you think the dime did not stick to the magnet?" Guide students to realize that the paper clip is made from metal that is magnetic, and the dime is made from metal that is not magnetic.

STEP 6

Challenge each student to search the room with a magnet to find other objects made from metals that are magnetic. Caution students not to put a magnet on any electronics, such as a computer or television, because it could harm the items.

This Is Why

A magnet is a piece of metal that has an invisible force called magnetism. Magnetism attracts certain kinds of metals to a magnet: iron, steel, cobalt, and nickel. Objects made from these metals are magnetic materials.

What Now?

Help students understand that magnets can attract or repel each other. Explain that there is a north pole and a south pole on opposite ends of a magnet. If the north and south poles of two magnets are near each other, they will attract and stick together. If the two poles are the same, the magnets will repel, pushing away from each other.

More About Magnets

Magnetism on the Move

Exploring magnetic force

Students discover firsthand how magnetic force can move objects through some nonmagnetic materials! Invite a child to hold a paper plate with a paper clip placed on top. Have another student slide a magnet along the underside of the plate, showing how the magnetic force works through the plate to move the paper clip. Challenge students to predict what will happen if they try the same experiment using other materials such as a book or a block of wood. Have them test their predictions and compare the results. Lead students to understand that the further apart the object and the magnet are, the weaker the magnetic force.

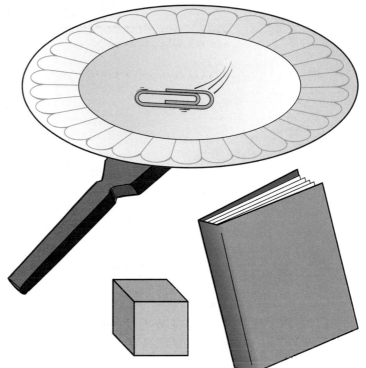

Get Magnetized!

Exploring magnetic strength

This activity shows youngsters how magnetic materials can become magnetized too! Invite each child, in turn, to place a paper clip on the end of a magnet. Have her touch the end of the paper clip to a second paper clip to see how it sticks to the first one. Challenge her to make a chain of paper clips as long as possible. Have her predict what will happen if she removes the first paper clip from the magnet. Invite her to test her prediction and compare the results. Guide students to understand that when a magnetic material is attracted to a magnet it becomes magnetized, but the object will lose its magnetic power when it is no longer touching the magnet.

Magnetic Attraction

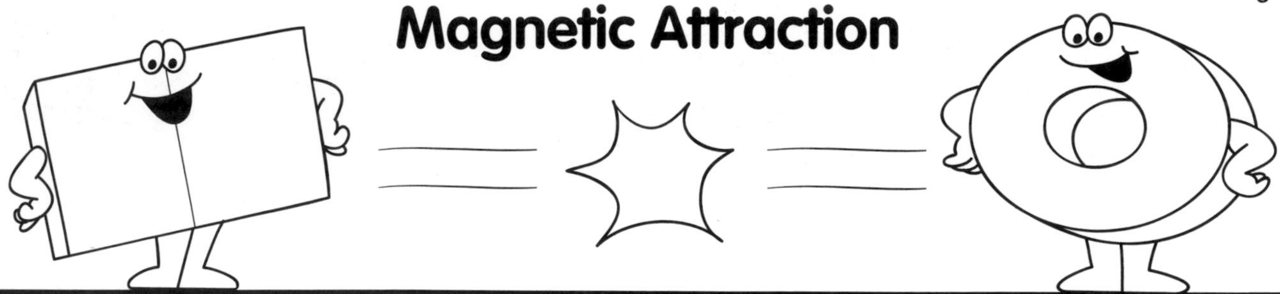

I think the magnet will be attracted to the

_____.

I think the magnet will be attracted to the

_____.

Did the object stick to the magnet?

☐ Yes   ☐ No

Did the object stick to the magnet?

☐ Yes   ☐ No

Is the object made from magnetic material?

☐ Yes   ☐ No

Is the object made from magnetic material?

☐ Yes   ☐ No

Let's Do Science Today! • ©The Mailbox® Books • TEC61165

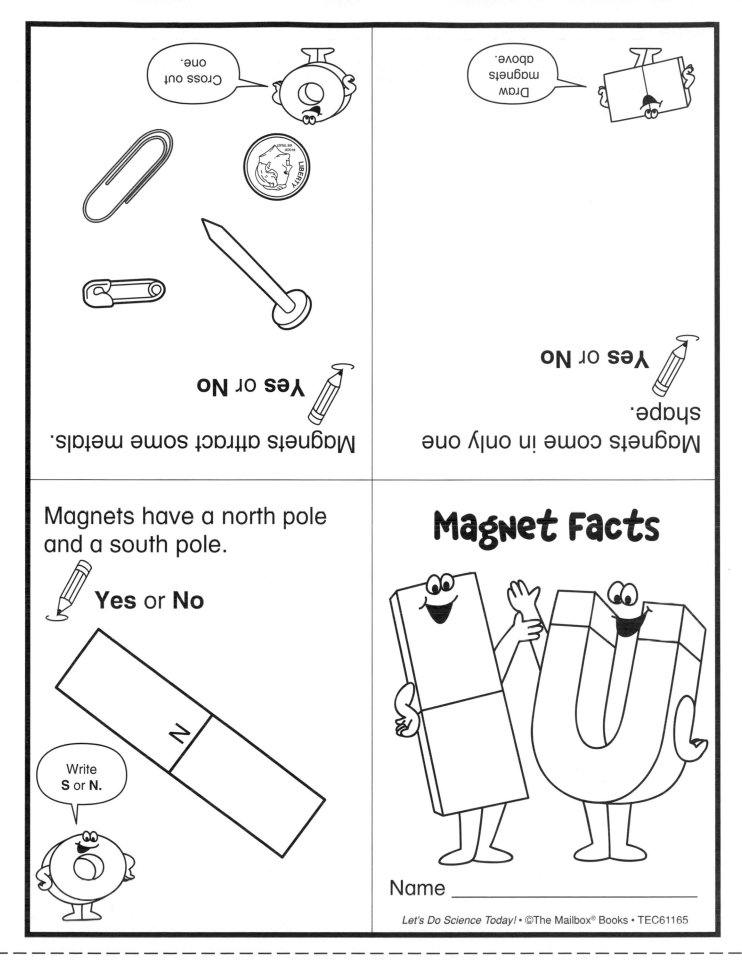

Cross out one.

Yes or **No**

Magnets attract some metals.

Draw magnets above.

Yes or **No**

Magnets come in only one shape.

Magnets have a north pole and a south pole.

Yes or **No**

Write **S** or **N.**

N

Magnet Facts

Name _____

Let's Do Science Today! • ©The Mailbox® Books • TEC61165

Fold-and-Go Booklet: To make a booklet, cut on the bold line. Fold along the thin horizontal line (keeping the programming to the outside) and then fold along the thin vertical line (keeping the cover to the outside). Read aloud each booklet page and have each child follow the directions to complete the booklet.

75

Key Science Learning
Pushes and pulls are forces that make things move.

During the investigation, students

● discover how people use force to move their bodies

● push and pull objects to make them move

● experience the need for a stronger force to move heavier objects

Materials:
tub of blocks
beanbag per student pair

In advance: Within student reach, put one block next to the tub of blocks.

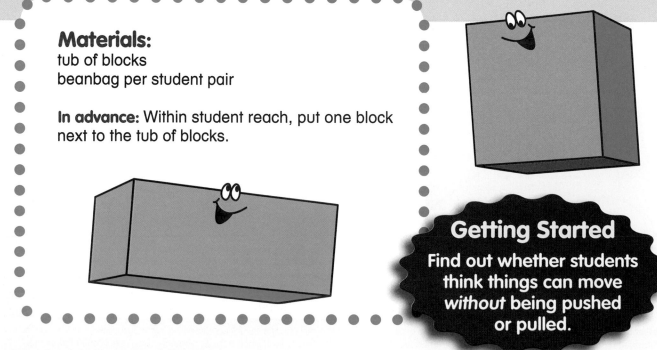

Getting Started
Find out whether students think things can move *without* being pushed or pulled.

STEP 1

Start by asking, "When we walk, do we push or pull anything to help us move?" After students respond, have them stand to discover how we move. Guide youngsters to understand that we push the ground or floor with our feet to make us move.

STEP 2

In pairs, have one student pick up a beanbag and toss it to his partner. Then have the partner drop the beanbag, pick it up, and toss it to her partner.

STEP 3

Ask, "How did the beanbag move?" Lead students to conclude that when you lift something, you are pulling it up; when you throw something, you are pushing it away.

STEP 4

Recap that pushes and pulls make things move. Have each student, in turn, push and pull the block and then push and pull the tub of blocks.

Investigation
Push and Pull

STEP 5

"It was easy to move the block."

"The tub was heavy and hard to move."

Ask, "What did you notice when you moved each object?" Then explain that heavy objects require a stronger push or pull (more force) to move than lighter objects.

STEP 6

"When it rains, water pushes dirt."

Challenge students to give examples of other ways things are pushed and pulled. Lead youngsters to conclude that an object does not move without force, a push or a pull.

Did You Know?

Two forces that stop objects from moving are friction and gravity. Friction is the force that slows things down when they rub against each other, and gravity is the force that pulls things down. Without air friction and gravity, as in outer space, an object that is pushed will keep moving forever, unless it bumps into something!

What Now?

Go outside and encourage youngsters to identify things that are moving. For each sighting, help them name the force that is responsible for the movement.

Squash and Stretch!

Exploring push and pull movements

Give each student a ball of play dough. Remind students that a push and a pull are forces that make things move. After rolling the ball forward and back with pushes and pulls, explore some more by having each child push down on the play dough. Discuss how a push will squash some things. Then have youngsters pull the play dough. Lead students to conclude that a pull will stretch some things. If desired, go a step further and explore with other materials, such as a rubber band, an air-filled balloon, a sponge ball, and a piece of aluminum foil.

I push and pull when I put on my boots.

Raheem

I push and pull when I brush my teeth.

Melissa

Get Moving!

Writing

Real-world pushing and pulling experiences are sure to make a great class book! Brainstorm with students activities that include pushing and pulling. Then give each child a sheet of paper and help her write about one activity that includes pulling and/or pushing movements. Next, instruct her to illustrate her sentence on her paper. Staple the pages together to make a class book.

Make It Move!

Look at each picture.

 Circle.

pull   both

push

pull   both

push

pull   both

push

pull   both

push